William Martin

Inquiries Concerning the Structure of the Semitic Languages

Part II

William Martin

Inquiries Concerning the Structure of the Semitic Languages
Part II

ISBN/EAN: 9783337062927

Printed in Europe, USA, Canada, Australia, Japan

Cover: Foto ©Thomas Meinert / pixelio.de

More available books at **www.hansebooks.com**

INQUIRIES

CONCERNING THE STRUCTURE

OF THE

SEMITIC LANGUAGES.

PART II.

BY

SIR W. MARTIN, D.C.L.

WILLIAMS AND NORGATE,
14, HENRIETTA STREET, COVENT GARDEN, LONDON;
AND 20, SOUTH FREDERICK STREET, EDINBURGH.
1878.

HERTFORD:
PRINTED BY STEPHEN AUSTIN AND SONS.

PREFACE.

To this second and concluding Part of these inquiries it appears to be necessary to prefix a few remarks, in order to make more clear the plan and object of the book.

1. In the former Part, the writer began by laying down certain propositions comprising (it is believed) the main principles by which the construction or Syntax of the Hebrew language is regulated, and by citing in support of each proposition a number of examples. Thence the inquiry proceeded through the whole series of the Historical Books, as they stand in the Hebrew Bible, up to and including the Books of Kings. In those Books various passages were noted to which the principles so laid down were applied. It appeared to the writer that the result was to bring out with greater distinctness and force the meaning of the text; and,

further, that no passage was found of which the structure was inconsistent with those principles.

So far, the inquiry was conducted with the advantage, in almost every case, of a clear context. There was little difficulty in verifying or justifying, by aid of that context, the effect which, according to the principles before laid down, was to be assigned to the Verbal Form in each case; so as to determine the proper historical time, past, present, or future, of each fact or event, and also its relation to other facts or events referred to in the narrative.

2. On entering on the Book of *Psalms* the case was changed. There, the narration of facts gives place to an expression of the varying feelings of each Psalmist as he looks before and after; oftentimes shifting his view suddenly, and passing through rapid changes and contrasts of thought and feeling. In this Book, then, was found a sufficient, even a severe, test of the rules laid down. And, those rules being (as is believed) strictly and faithfully applied to the Psalms, the rendering so attained is found to furnish a clear and connected sense. This result appears to establish the soundness of the principles themselves; and also to give reason to expect that a similar result will follow upon the

application of the same rules to the remaining poetical Books of Scripture.

If this is indeed within reach, if it is possible to determine the true rendering of the Hebrew Text by a fair and unforced application of grammatical rules, we may hope to be relieved from much that is arbitrary, and much that is conjectural, in the current criticism of the Old Testament.

3. It may be hoped also that some few persons will be moved to investigate for themselves these questions. It may reasonably be believed that the imperfection of our ordinary treatises on the Hebrew Speech was among the causes of the indifference to these studies which has long prevailed in England. The grammatical forms of words were fully explained in those treatises: not so, the forms of thought, and the devices by which the relations of thought to thought are expressed. The student was able to verify the English Version, word by word; but at that point he commonly stopped. Indeed, few persons will persevere in the reading of a book in a strange tongue, if they are unable to go further than that; if, after all, they feel themselves unable to determine, on some trustworthy grounds, the true and precise meaning of the author. It may then be

hoped that the ascertainment and verification of clear and definite rules of Syntax may tend to a renewed interest in studies which, to our great loss, have been so long neglected.

4. In all such investigations as these, of which the result is now before the reader, there is of course much room for error; partly from the intrinsic difficulty of the subject, and partly from the infirmity of the human mind. Men are disposed to love their own thoughts, as their own children; often, very unwisely. All that can be done is to leave the whole matter (as it is now left) to the judgment of competent and candid persons, and to time.

In this second Part, it is shown that the principles, before laid down as to the Forms of the Hebrew Verb, apply also to the Forms of the Arabic Verb. An attempt is also made to exhibit the mode in which the tri-consonantal Verbs (both Hebrew and Arabic) are built up from simple roots.

The object of the fourth Inquiry is to show that certain passages, which have been supposed to form exceptions to one of the main rules of the Hebrew language, do not really involve any departure from that rule.

The remaining Inquiries relate to matters (less closely connected with the main subject) in respect of which there appears to be reason to doubt the accuracy of renderings, which have found, of late years, a certain degree of acceptance among Hebrew scholars.

In order to compare the several dialects, it has been found necessary to adopt, as far as practicable, one common mode of writing for all; seeing that many scholars, possessing a fair acquaintance with the Hebrew, are not familiar with the characters in which the other dialects are written.

The use of a European alphabet for writing the Semitic tongues has been recently recommended by high authority on more general grounds. At the Congress of Orientalists, held at London in 1874, the President (Dr. S. Birch, of the British Museum) expressed his conviction that, for most Oriental languages, the adoption of some one mode of transliteration would be of the highest importance; and that, not merely as superseding the necessity of an expensive and difficult process of printing in various characters. "It is evident," he said, "that, clothed in a European alphabet, there would be no greater difficulty in mastering many of the Aryan and Semitic languages by the Western scholars than in acquiring the different languages spoken in Europe —a task much facilitated by their having one common mode of printing and writing the same sounds."

In the following pages each of the letters of the original Arabic alphabet is represented by the character or sign which has been employed in the former Part, as an equivalent for the corresponding Hebrew or Syriac letter.

The letters, *Kha*, *Dhal*, *Dsad*, *Gain*, are represented by $\dot{\chi}$, δ, z, γ.

INDEX

	PAGE
PREFACE	v
I.—FORMS OF THE ARABIC VERB	1
II.—SEMITIC ROOTS	9
III.—REDUPLICATE FORMS	23
IV.—ON THE GRAMMATICAL STRUCTURE OF JOEL, CHAP. II.	33
V.—ON SOME USES OF THE PARTICLE $e\theta$	43
VI.—THE DIVINE NAME	49

ERRATA IN PART I.

p. 12. The lines 2–4 should be omitted.

p. 13. The lines 3–7 should be transferred to p. 22, and placed immediately after line 8.

SEMITIC INQUIRIES.

PART II.

I.

FORMS OF THE ARABIC VERB.

THE object of this Essay is to show that the use of the Forms of the Verb is regulated in Arabic by the same general principles as have been laid down in reference to the Hebrew Verb in the former part of these inquiries.

THE IMPERFECT.

1. The *Imperfect* is used, in *independent* sentences or clauses, to express acts or events which are regarded as transitory or incomplete, commencing at some particular point of time, or continuing during some interval of time, past, present, or future. It may be a single act; or a recurring act; or an act expected to occur in a certain state of things, whenever that may arise.

EXAMPLES.

"Man *proposes*, God *disposes*" (yudabbaru—yuḳaddaru); *i.e.* Of every single act which man proposes at any time, God determines the issue.

Loḳmān, Fab. 7. "A man *is not justified* by the testimony of his family" (mā yuzakkaˏ); *i.e.* If at any time an accusation is brought against a man, he is not cleared at that time by such testimony alone.

2. So far is the Arabic Imperfect from indicating in itself a future time (according to the theory of the old grammars), that a special form has been devised, and is in constant use, for the purpose of distinguishing the cases in which the Imperfect is to be understood as indicating an event wholly future; namely, the placing of the noun *sawf*, or of its initial letter *s*, immediately before the Imperfect.

EXAMPLE.

Ḳor.[1] vi. 5. "*Then in the end* the message, at which they mocked, shall *overtake them*" (fa-sawfa—yā atī-him).

3. The Imperfect takes the time indicated by the context.

EXAMPLES.

Ḳor. vi. 130. "Came not Apostles to you, *warning you?*" (yundirūna-kum).

---

[1] In quotations from the Ḳorān, the version of Rev. J. M. Rodwell is followed.

Ḳor. xii. 16. "They came to their father *weeping*" (yabkūna).

In the three instances following, the same words, 'lā yaṣʿurūna,' are used: in the two former in a past sense; in the last in a future sense.

Ḳor. xvi. 28. "They who were before them did plot of old. Then God attacked their building at its foundation;—and, *whence they looked not for it*, punishment overtook them." (lā yaṣʿurūna).

Ḳor. vii. 93. "Therefore did we seize upon them suddenly, *when they were unaware.*" (wa-hum lā yaṣʿurūna).

Ḳor. xii. 107. "Are they sure that God's day of doom shall not come upon them suddenly, *while they are unaware?*" (wa-hum lā yaṣʿurūna), *i.e.* they not being aware at that future time.

PERFECT.

4. The *Perfect* is used, in *independent* sentences or clauses, to express states, conditions, or relations which are regarded as complete and abiding, belonging to no particular point or interval of time: states of the human mind and feelings, habits or customs, course of life: offices, functions, or permanent relations: facts regarded as complete and entirely past: facts regarded as absolutely certain to happen.

EXAMPLES.

Ḳor. xii. 67. "In Him put I my trust (habitually)" (tawakkaltu).

Ḳor. vi. 98. "It is He who *sendeth down* rain from heaven." *i.e.* He is the sender down of rain (anzala).

Ḳor. vi. 115. "The words of thy Lord *are perfect.*" (tammat).

Ḳor. vi. 128–130. "And when God shall gather them together (*i.e.* Jinns and men)—their votaries *shall say*, 'O our Lord, we rendered one another services.'—He *will say*, 'Your abode the fire. Therein abide ye for ever, unless so God shall will.'—'O race of Jinn and men, came not Apostles to you from among yourselves, warning you of the meeting of this day?' They *shall say*, 'We bear witness against ourselves.'" (ḳāla—ḳāla—ḳālū).

Another example occurs in the same *Sura*, verse 30.

Ḳor. xiv. 24. "All mankind *shall come forth* before God; and the weak *shall say* to the men of pride, 'Verily we were your followers.'—They *shall say*, 'If God had guided us, we surely had guided you.'" (barazū—ḳala—ḳālu).

5. The Arabic *Perfect* is so far from indicating only a past time that a special device has been adopted for the purpose of indicating cases in which the Perfect is to be understood as expressing a time past: namely, the prefixing of the particle *ḳad* to the Perfect. The past time so expressed is such, either in reference to the actual present or to some other time, itself already past.

6. The following examples exhibit the contrast of the

senses in which the two forms of the same root are used.

Ḳor. lvii. 1. "All that is in the Heaven and in the Earth *praiseth* God; and He is the Mighty, the Wise." (sabbaχa).

Ḳor. xxiv. 36. "In the temples, which God hath allowed to be reared, do men *praise* Him *morn and even*." (yusabbiχū).

Ibid. 41. "*Hast thou not seen* how all in the Heavens and in the Earth *uttereth the praise* of God?—the very birds, as they spread their wings?" (yusabbiχū).

In the first of these examples, the Heavens and the Earth are conceived of as praising God, by testifying at *all times* to His power and wisdom. To express this conception the Perfect is used. In the second and third examples, the utterance of praise is conceived of as occurring at some specific time or times.

DEPENDENT CLAUSES.

7. In clauses expressing a close connexion or dependence of acts, the Imperfect Form is employed, ordinarily with the particle *li* prefixed:

Ḳor. xiv. 1. "This book have We sent down to thee, *that thou mayest bring* men *out* of darkness into light." (li—tuχrija).

Ḳor. vi. 145. "Who is more wicked than he who in his ignorance inventeth a lie against men *to deceive* men?" (li—yuẓilla).

Ḳor. xix. 97. "We have made this (Ḳorān) easy in thine own tongue, *that thou mayest announce glad tidings by it to the God-fearing.*" (li—tubassira).

Ḳor. vi. 14. "I am ordered *to be* (lit. *that I be*) the first of those who surrender themselves to God." (an akūna).

PARTICIPLE.

8. In Arabic, as in Hebrew, the so-called *Participle* (*nomen agentis* or *patientis*) does not convey in itself any notion of time past, present, or future. The time to which the action or condition belongs is to be gathered from the context.

EXAMPLES.

Ḳor. ix. 85. "Verily they believed not in God and His Apostles, and died *in their wickedness*" (*lit.* and *they evil doers*) (wa-hum fāsiḳūna).

Ḳor. xii. 13. "I fear lest the wolf devour him while *ye are heedless*" (lit. *and you unheeding*) (wa-antum γāfilūna).

NARRATIVE.

9. The form of Narrative, which was in use among the Hebrews in ancient times, has been set forth in the former part of these inquiries. In a later age, after the return from the Babylonian Captivity, when the official interpreters in the Synagogues of Palestine rendered the text of the Old Testament into the local dialect of their

own time, they did not attempt to follow closely the grammatical structure of the older language. Events which, whilst comparatively recent, had been vividly narrated and made present to the hearer or reader, had passed far away and become parts of ancient history. So the peculiar form of the old narratives was abandoned; the Perfect Form, which (as we have seen) had been used in the *Preface* to each of those Narratives, was now carried on throughout. The usage thus adopted in the Targums was followed by the Syriac translators of the Old Testament; and, in a later age, by the Arabic writers. Thus the particle of sequence, under its Arabic form *fa*, is ordinarily followed by a Perfect. Contrary, also, to Hebrew usage, the *fa* may be separated from its verb.

EXAMPLE.

Ḳor. vi. 75–79. "So did we show Abraham the domain of the Heavens and the Earth. *And*, when the night overshadowed him, he *beheld* a star; 'This,' said he, 'is my Lord;' but (or *then*), when it set, *he said*, 'I love not gods which set.' *And*, when he beheld the moon uprising, 'This,' said he, 'is my Lord;' *but*, when it set, he said, 'Surely if my Lord guide me not, I shall be of those who go astray.' *And*, when he beheld the sun uprise, *he said*, 'This is my Lord; this is greatest.' *But*, when it set, *he said*, 'O my people, I share not with you the guilt of joining gods with God.'"

In place of the words *and* and *but*, in italics in the

foregoing passage, there stands in the Arabic one and the same word *fa;* marking in every case a time later than that of the fact last before mentioned. The *fa* is in each case separated by intervening words from its verb (fa—raa̱,—fa—ḳūla, etc.).

10. It may be noticed that in Arabic there are some uses of this particle *fa,* to which there is nothing exactly corresponding in the use of the Hebrew *wa;* but in all cases the sense of *sequence* or *consequence* may be recognized.

II.

SEMITIC ROOTS.

1. In acquiring the ancient languages of the West, the student finds his labour diminished by the fact that many of the verbs are compounded of certain simpler verbs and of a limited number of prepositions. The simpler verbs being in frequent use, and the general meaning of each preposition being clear, it follows that the compound verb conveys or suggests at first sight the meaning which usage has assigned to it, or something approaching to that. On the contrary, in seeking to acquire the Semitic languages, the student meets with a large number of verbs apparently unconnected with one another. On a more careful examination, however, it is possible to detect in many cases a common element or primitive root, by joining to which certain prefixes or suffixes the ordinary verbs have been formed. This common element sometimes appears as a single consonant followed by a long vowel. More commonly it has two consonants. In such cases, these two consonants are, in Hebrew, united into one syllable by a short vowel interposed; in Arabic, each has its own short vowel, so

that the root becomes disyllabic. We may not be able to determine the specific meaning or force of these several prefixes or suffixes; but it is apparent that their function was to limit the large and vague meaning of the primitive root in such way that each of the fuller forms, so compounded, had a definite meaning of its own.

2. This mode of formation has been recognized by Gesenius, and by other lexicographers, and has been applied by him in some instances. It appears to be capable of a much wider application. All that is aimed at here is to show clearly the operation of this principle by a sufficient number of examples. No opinion is here offered, or involved, as to any of the ingenious and subtle theories which have been propounded by learned men, as to the primeval structure of human speech. Moreover, the inquiry is not extended to the Syriac dialect, owing to the great similarity of that dialect to the Hebrew. Though the roots of the Syriac often vary somewhat from those of the Hebrew, by reason of the interchange of consonants, the main principles of structure are alike in both dialects.

3. This kind of development from the primitive root did not proceed uniformly in the several dialects. In some cases the later forms, derived from one and the same root, are numerous in one dialect, scanty in another. But to whatever extent it might be carried, it was always in conformity with the principles above stated.

Also in the different dialects, in the shape in which

we now view them, the syllables used as roots, as well as those which are used as prefixes or suffixes, are liable to be varied according to certain general laws which regulate the interchange or transformation of consonants in those dialects.

4. Towards discerning and distinguishing the Semitic roots, we derive especial aid from the Arabic. For the more complete alphabet of the Arabs represents, by appropriate characters, sounds which in the Hebrew alphabet are confounded under one character. Thus, the Hebrew character *Zain* includes two sounds, which are represented in the Arabic alphabet by the characters *Za* and *Dha*, and herein by z and δ (=the *th* in *thou*); the Hebrew letter *Heth* comprises the Arabic letters *Hha* and *Kha*, herein written χ and $\dot{\chi}$; the Hebrew ṣ, the Arabic ṣ (=*ts*), and ẓ (=*dz*); the Hebrew *Ain* covers the Arabic *'Ain* (ʿ), and *Gain* γ (resembling the modern Greek pronunciation of the γ in the word ἀγάπη).

With this help, it has become practicable in many cases to separate into distinct groups the diverse meanings which, in our Hebrew Dictionaries, are usually placed under one heading; and to assign each group to its own proper root.

5. The following examples will serve to show the way in which a common bi-consonantal root reappears under various disguises in the different Semitic dialects.

The significations here assigned to the Hebrew words are taken from *Gesenius*; those assigned to the Arabic words, from *Freitag*.

I.

baṭ *(Hebrew)*.

bāṭ-aχ = confisus est alicui; spem et fiduciam in aliquem conjecit. (*Arab.* baṭa-χa, *prostravit resupinum;* conjecit in faciem: unde Hebr. *bāṭaχ bĕ,* fort. pr. conjecit se *vel* curas suas in aliquem).

beṭ-aχ = fiducia, securitas.

biṭ-χāh (biṭ-tāχōn) = fiducia, spes.

būṭ-ūaχ = confisus (*significatione activa*).

shē-veṭ (she-veṭ) baculus, virga, sceptrum, hasta: tribus (a sceptro ducis).

χa-vaṭ = fuste decussit, excussit, *poma olivasque de arbore decussit.*

nā-vaṭ (inusit). *Hif.* hib-bīṭ = spectavit, intuitus est.

baṭa *(Arabic)*.

baṭa-χa = projecit in faciem ac pronum.

ha-baṭa = decidit, *a monte.* 4. demisit, dejecit; diminuit *pretium rei.*

wa-baṭa = debilis fuit, vilis fuit.

χa-baṭa = frustra et sine præmio fuit opus.

baṭa-la = vanus, nihil, frustra et incassum, fuit *vel* evasit.

The original force then of this root was to indicate a *throwing* or *casting down;* out of which vague and general meaning were developed, by means of certain prefixes or suffixes, specific terms to indicate the following acts or objects of thought:

a. A rod or *lance*; the lance, borne in the hand of each ruler of a tribe (σκηπτοῦχοι βασιλῆες), naturally coming to express a *tribe*.

b. To *cast oneself* upon another, seeking from him help or protection; to trust in him.

c. To *come down, fall in value*, to be low, cheap, vain, or worthless.

The connexion of the Hebrew form 'hib-bīṭ' with this root will be shown below.

II.

χav *(Hebrew)*.

χāv-al = ligavit, funem adstrinxit; whence χib-bēl = *pignore* adstrinxit.
χāv-ash = ligavit, alligavit, obligavit.
χev-el = funis, funiculus, caterva hominum.
χōvēl = nauta (a χevel).
χāv-ar = conjunctus est, cohæsit.
χev-er = conjunctio, societas.
χāv-er = sodalis, socius.
χāv-av = amavit.
χōv-ereθ = conjunctio, commissura.
χav-ōl = pignus.

χaba *(Arabic)*.

χaba-sa = retinuit, continuit. IV. in vincula carceremve conjecit.

χaba-la = laqueo cepit *feram;* fune strinxit; fœdus inivit; securitatem invenit.
χab-l = funis, chorda, vinculum, amicitia.
sa-χiba = socius *aut* comes fuit alicui.
sa-χīb = socius.
na-χaba = vovit, votum fecit; certavit deposito pignore, sponsione facta. VI. constituerunt invicem tempus alicui rei.
wa-χaba = debere, seu decere, competere.

The primary notion conveyed by this root is plainly that of *binding*. The derived forms express the several modes of binding: *a.* by means of a rope or chain; *b.* by a tie of love, affection, or companionship; *c.* by a promise or compact; by a vow; by an obligation or debt; much in the same way as we use the derivatives of the word *bind*, viz. *band, bond, bounden*.

It should be noticed, that the Hebrew verb χāvā or χāvāh, *abscondit*, which is commonly classed with the words enumerated above, belongs rather to the same class as the Arabic χabaa = *occultavit*.

III.

kan *(Hebrew)*.

kāna' = depressa fuit terra; depressus est animus.
shū-kan = subsedit, cubuit, quievit, habitavit.
kēn = *n.* locus, basis; *adj.* probus, integer.
sā-kan = habitavit; pauper, egenus, fuit.
kūn (inusit.) Inde nā-kōn = firmus, constans, fundatus.

mā-kōn = locus (maxime de *loco*, i.e. de habitatione, domicilio, *Dei*), fundamentum, basis.

kōn-ēn = confirmavit, sustentavit, fundavit (*urbem, terram, cœlum*).

kana *(Arabic)*.

sa-kana = quietus, tranquillus, fuit; habitavit domum.
mis-kīn = pauper, egenus.
kāna = accidit res, exstitit. X. submisit et humiliavit se.
kawn = essentia, existentia.
ma-kān = locus ubi quid exstitit.

The primitive root conveyed the meaning of *being placed low*, or *on the ground*.

Hence were derived forms to indicate a low land; depression of mind; the going down of a wind; the condition of a man brought low or reduced to poverty.

Other forms had the signification of being founded on the ground; of being fixed, established; of a permanent existence; of an abiding fact.

IV.

saf *(Hebrew)*.

sūf = rapere, auferre. *Hif.* sustulit e medio, finem fecit. *Intrans.* cessare, desinere.
sūf-āh = turbo cuncta secum abripiens.
sāf-āh = abrasit, abstulit vitam. *Intrans.* sublatus est, periit.

ā-saf = rasit, corrasit. 1. collegit *fruges*; congregavit *homines, populos;* 2. recepit apud se; 3. collegit ad se, contraxit, retraxit.

ă-saf-suf = collectus; turba miscella, colluvies.

yā-saf = addidit, auxit.

sāf-ar = scripsit. *part.* sōfēr; scriba, *tribunus militum* qui exercitui conscribendo præfectus est; numeravit.

safa *(Arabic)*.

safa-ra = 1. Verrit domum. 2. Dimovit, remomovit, *ut ventus nubes e cœlo*.

safū (*i.e.* safa-a) Agilis ac velox fuit eundo vel volando; abripuit, dispersit, asportavit *pulverem ventus*.

The original meaning of *safa* is to *sweep*. Thence are derived words meaning to sweep together; to gather corn into a granary; to bring persons into a place of safety; to bring stray cattle home to their owner: also, to collect; to add together; to make a list or register (sēfer), *e.g.* of ancestors or of fighting men: again, to sweep away; to make an end of a thing.

N.B.—The Arabic verb *safara* has also other meanings, which are to be explained by referring them to a root *fara* with the prefix *sa*.

V.

ṣar *(Hebrew)*.

ṣūr = coarctare, premere, comprimere. Inde 1. colligare in *sarcinam, volumen;* 2. obsidere urbem; 3. urgere, insistere *alicui in persequendo;* 4. secare, dividere; 5. fingere, *i.q.* yāṣar (a secando ductum). Arab. ṣawwara *id.*

ṣūr=lapis, silex (ita dictus, utpote massa coacta, compacta): rupes; acies ensis.

ā-ṣar=recondidit reposuit, reposuit in thesauro. (Origo est in claudendo, includendo, coercendo. Cf. radices cognatas χaṣar, ʿaṣar.)

χā-ṣar *rad. inusit.* unde χiṣār (Arab.)=sepimentum, munimentum, castellum.

χā-ṣēr=septum, locus septo circumdatus.

nā-ṣar=custodivit, tuitus est, defendit.

ʿā-ṣar=clausit; (origo est in circumdando circumvallo.)

yā-ṣar=finxit, formavit, *ut figulus lutum, artifex statuas.* Sed *intrans.* coarctatus, angustus fuit.

ṣār-ar=1. pressit, compressit; constrinxit, colligavit; 2. corripuit; 3. inclusit; 4. pressit, persecutus est.

ṣara *(Arabic).*

a-ṣara=ligavit; inclusit, continuit, coercuit.

χa-ṣara=in angustiam redegit; circumdederunt *homines aliquem,* eum capturi.

χi-ṣār=sepimentum, munimentum, castellum.

χa-ṣūr (*i.q.* χa-ṣīr)=angusto pectore præditus.

ṣar-ra=constrinxit, nodavitque *crumenam.*

ʿa-ṣara=pressit uvas, expressit succum.

This root *ṣar* conveys the notion of *narrowness, tightness, extreme closeness.*

Thence are derived words meaning to confine within a narrow space, to press close, to bind tightly together, to shut in or inclose.

From the noun *ṣūr=silex* we have the verb ṣūr in the sense of cutting or fashioning with a knife or edged tool.

N.B.—The meaning *hostiliter tractavit, æmulatus est, zelotypus fuit*, assigned by Gesenius to the Hebrew ṣar-ar, belongs (as Gesenius himself points out) to the Arabic root ẓar-ra, which Freitag explains by *nocuit, noxa affecit*.

VI.

ḳal *(Hebrew)*.

ḳal=levis.
ḳal-al=levis fuit; vilis, contemtus fuit.
sū-ḳal=libravit, pependit; appendit *alicui*.
se-ḳel=siclus, certum auri argentique pondus, quo appenso pro moneta utebantur Hebræi. Comp. *pondus* et *pondo*.

ḳala *(Arabic)*.

ḳal-la=paucus fuit; paucum esse aliquid declaravit; sustulit in se portavitque.
θa-ḳala=gravitatem et pondus exploravit. II. gravem et ponderosum reddidit.

The simple root *ḳal* indicates something *light* or easily lifted. Thence are derived words to express the act of lifting (or *weighing* in the old sense, *e.g.* to weigh anchor); of *weighing* in the ordinary sense; and of *weight*.

VII.

rag *(Hebrew).*

ā-rag=plexit, texuit (inde Gr. ἀράχνη). Primaria hujus radicis syllaba est *rag* quæ *motionis celerisque agitationis* potestatem habebat. Cf. *rajja* (Arab.), *movit, agitavit.*

hā-rag=interfecit; de cæde quacunque, sive gladio committitur, sive saxo conjecto.

χā-rag=tremuit, trepidavit.

nā-rag=celeriter locutus est.

śa-rag=plexit, implexit.

rāg-az=commotus est, perturbatus est, contremuit, trepidavit.

rāg-as=strepuit, tumultuatus est.

raja *(Arabic).*

raj-ja=movit, agitavit, tremefecit.

raja-fa=commovit; vehementer commotus est, vacillavit.

naw-raja=horsum ac prorsum se vertit *in incessu, in sermone.*

From the root *rag* or Arabic *raja* (which conveys a notion of swift and repeated movement) are derived words to express the act of plying the shuttle; of speaking rapidly; of slaying or destroying by repeated strokes; of the destruction of vines by hailstones; of the movements of an excited crowd; of the tumultuous stir of a great festival.

6. A further advantage to be derived from a careful observation of these primitive Semitic roots is this: that clear and specific distinctions will often show themselves between Hebrew words which are apt to be rendered by the same English words; and thereby the true force of many passages of the Hebrew text will become apparent. For example, the use of each of the Hebrew words χàzāh and *hibbiṭ* will be seen to correspond accurately with the meaning of its root.

The root of χāzāh is χaz, which appears in the common verb ā-χaz=*prehendit, cepit, prehensum tenuit*. In the Syriac dialect this root assumes the form χad; in the Arabic, χaδ. Under all these forms the meaning remains the same.

In accordance with this radical meaning we find χāzāh used to express the *fixed* gaze of a *beholder*, who sees before him some vast or awful object.

EXAMPLES.

Psalm xlvi. 9. "Come, *behold* the works of the Lord, what desolations He hath wrought upon the earth." (χăzū).

Exodus xxiv. 11. "They *saw* God, and did eat and drink" (yeχĕzū).

Numbers xxiv. 4. "He hath said, which heard the words of God, which *saw the vision* of the Almighty." (yeχĕzeh—maχăzēh).

Isaiah i. 1. "The *vision* of Isaiah ... which he *saw*." (χăzōn—χāzāh).

The prophet himself, the Seer, is χōzeh.

On the other hand, the verb *hibbīṭ* (in the Hif. or causative form) denotes a conscious act: a directing of the eyes towards an object; a look shifting from one object to another: a look which follows the course of an object in motion.

EXAMPLES.

Genesis xv. 5. "And He brought him forth abroad, and said, *Look*. now toward heaven, and tell the stars." (habbēṭ-nā).

Genesis xix. 26. "His wife *looked back* from behind him." (tabbēṭ).

Exodus xxxiii. 8. "When Moses went out unto the tabernacle, all the people rose up and stood and *looked after* Moses, until he was gone into the tabernacle." (hibbīṭū).

Numbers xii. 8. "The similitude of the Lord shall he behold"; rather he shall have a view—yet a passing or momentary view—of that similitude (yabbīṭ).

Psalm civ. 32. "He *looketh on* the earth, and it trembleth: He *toucheth* the hills and they smoke."

In this example the parallelism of the two clauses—*ham-mabbīṭ* being set over against *yiggaʿ*—shows that the look is not a fixed and continuing look, but rather a momentary one, a glance.

Isaiah lxiii. 5. "I *looked* (from side to side) and there was none to help" (abbīṭ).

Isaiah lxvi. 1, 2. "Thus saith the Lord, the heaven is my throne, and the earth is my footstool: where is the house that ye build unto me? All those things hath my hand made; but to this man *will I look*, to him that is poor and of a contrite heart." (abbīṭ) *i.e.* From heaven and earth, from the holy place, I will turn mine eyes to the poor and contrite man.

Job xxxix. 28, 29. "She (the eagle) dwelleth and abideth upon the rock, upon the crag of the rock. From thence she seeketh the prey, and her eyes behold afar off." *i.e.* The crag is her haunt, from which she *habitually spies out* her prey. (Hence the Perfect χāfar.) While she rests on the crag; her eyes *are glancing* hither and thither over the region below (yabbīṭū).

III.

REDUPLICATE FORMS.

1. In the Semitic dialects we find a considerable variety of verbal forms, in which some reduplication of the consonants of the root takes place; for example, *kirkēr* (=saltavit) from *kārar*. These forms resemble the intensive conjugation (Pi·ēl); and, like that conjugation, prefix the syllable *mĕ* to their Participle or *nomen agentis*, e.g. *mĕkarkēr* from *kirkēr* (II. Samuel vi. 14, 16).

In the present inquiry we are concerned with one class only of these forms, namely, that in which the primitive biconsonantal root alone is repeated, without any change of vowel. Verbs of this class resemble the conjugation, which is called by the grammarians 'Ḳal.'

The root is never repeated more than once. The repetition, once made, stands for an indefinite repetition of the motion or act expressed by the root; just as, at an earlier stage of the representation of human thought by visible signs, two wavy lines sufficed to represent, not two waves only of the sea, but even the whole sea.

2. The Arabic dialect furnishes a number of examples where a monosyllabic root is repeated simply. Thus from

zala comes *zal-zala* = commovit, tremefecit *Deus terram;* from *raja, raj-raja* = agitatus fuit, tremuit, vacillavit; from *rafa* (the root of the Arabic verb *rafa-ʿa*=in altum sustulit, elevavit; and *sha-rafa* = altus fuit, eminuit), *raf-rafa*=alas expandit; movit alas circum rem, in eam se immissurus *struthiocamelus;* from *ʿasa, ʿas-ʿasa*=appropinquavit terræ *nubes*, tenebrascere cœpit *nox*.

In Hebrew the monosyllabic root rarely occurs by itself. The reduplication presents itself for the most part in disyllabic verbs, of which the former syllable is a prefix. Of this prefix the consonant is retained, whilst its vowel is reduced to its shortest equivalent, in order to compensate for the increased length of the word, owing to the reduplication. Thus from sā-χar (circumivit, peragravit) is formed sĕ-χar-χar=cito circuivit cor, *i.e.* vehementer palpitavit.

3. These repeated acts are not to be viewed as acts distinct and separate from one another; the bringing of them together within the compass of one word indicates that all the repeated acts, comprised within that word, are parts of one and the same movement or operation.

Thus the reduplicate verb *zalzala* expresses the effect of a shock of earthquake in producing repeated vibrations or tremulous movements of the ground. The verb *raf-rafa* expresses the repeated efforts, which issue in the bird's act of lifting itself into the air. The verb *ʿas-ʿasa* expresses the gradual approach of the night, when every minute seems to add to the darkness; that is to say, the several stages of which the result is summed up in the verb ʿasā (ʿasa-a) = valde obscura fuit nox.

In the case of reduplicate *nouns* or *adjectives*, the notion of *movement*, inherent in the reduplicate verb, disappears; and that of a *state* of things or a *quality* takes its place. Thus from sāfar, Hebrew = *splenduit* (or rather from the Chaldee form sĕfar), we have sĕfarfārāh = aurora, Dan. vi. 20; from χālak = glaber, lævis fuit, we have χă-lak-lak-kōθ = loca lubrica.

So, from sā-χar = niger fuit, is derived se-χar-χar (*fem.* sĕ-χar-χōreθ = subnigra); from ā-dam = rubuit, ā-dam-dam = subruber; from yārak = viruit herba, yĕ-rak-rak = subviridis, subflavus. Whilst *niger, ruber, viridis*, are expressed by ā-dōm, sā-χōr, yārok.

Thus each *colour* is conceived of as passing through a series of stages, represented by the reduplicate form, before it reaches the complete or final state which is expressed by the unreduplicate form.

4. In Leviticus xvi. a word occurs which has given rise to much discussion and to wide difference of opinion among Hebrew scholars, namely, the word ʿAzā-zēl. This has been, no doubt, rightly regarded by Gesenius as a softened form of ʿA-zalzēl. Changes of this sort are to be observed in other cases: *e.g.* in kō-kav (stella) for kav-kav; in χă-ṣō-ṣer-āh (tuba) for χă-ṣar-ser-āh; and particularly in ē-ṣel (ad latus, juxta) for el-ṣelaʿ. This ʿā-zal-zēl is obviously a derivative from the verb ʿā-zal; a verb which does not occur elsewhere in the Old Testament, though other derivatives from the primitive root zal do

occur therein: *e.g. ā-zal*=abiit, discessit; *zal-al*=concussit, quassavit; effudit, profudit *saccum quasi excutiendo*; *zŭl* i.q. *zāl-al*; *nā-zal*=fluxit, manavit; defecit *aqua, cibus*. The Arabic supplies (besides *zal-zala* mentioned above) *zal-la*=lapsavit in loco lubrico, abiit *vita*; præteriit, transiit celeriter *vir*; *na-zala*=descendit *loco*, descendit *ex equo*. Moreover, it supplies the very word we have to deal with, namely, *ʿa-zala*=semovit, dimovit a *provincia*. II. semovit, dimovit. IV. semovit.

5. This particular form *ʿā-zal-zēl* appears to have been taken by the old interpreters to be a participle or participial noun; though their renderings, for the most part (ἀπερχόμενος—ἀπολελύμενος—ἀποπεμπόμενος—emissarius), fail to express the active force of the root *ʿāzal*. This active force seems to have been intended to be expressed by the LXX. in their use of the term ἀποπομπαῖος, and of the phrase εἰς τὴν ἀποπομπήν. Though examples of the active participle of the reduplicate form under consideration are wanting, an instance of the passive participle is found in Num. xi. 4, namely, the word *ʿa-saf-suf*=m. *collectus*, from the root *ā-saf*. This word is explained by Gesenius as 'turba miscella ex variis hominum generibus corrasa; *colluvies* quæ Israelitis se conjunxerat.' The true and literal meaning of the word obviously being this, "the body of men which was swept along with itself from time to time by the Israelitish host on its march." It may be inferred that the active participle, equivalent to *colligens* or *collector*, would be *ă-saf-sēf*. The corresponding derivative from *ʿā-zal* would be *ʿā-zal-zēl*.

6. We thus arrive at the grammatical force of *ă-zal-zêl*. The act of *removing* or *putting aside* or *separating off* is expressed, in the general and without modification, by the word *a-zal;* so the operation of removal or separation, when it is effected by a series of repeated acts, is rightly expressed by the word *ă-zal-zal*. In this sense the word *a-zā-zēl* is strictly expressive of the function which is ascribed to the scape-goat in vv. 21, 22; namely, that he " be sent away, bearing upon him all the iniquities of the children of Israel into the wilderness." It properly denotes one that removes or separates; yet a remover in such sort that the removal is not effected by a single act or at one moment, but by a series of minor acts tending to, and issuing in, a complete removal. No word could better express the movement of the goat before the eyes of the people, as it passed on removing at each step, in a visible symbol, their sins farther and farther from them, until, by continued repetition of the movement, they were carried far away and removed utterly.

7. To the view here taken, it is objected that the application of the word *azāzēl*, to the goat itself involves the Hebrew text in insuperable difficulties. Whether this objection is sound, may be determined by giving a literal rendering of the verses in which the word occurs, namely, v. 8, v. 10, in which it occurs twice, and v. 26.

v. 8. "And Aaron shall cast lots upon the two goats; one lot for the Lord, and one lot for a Remover (of sins)."

vv. 9, 10. "And Aaron shall bring in the goat upon which fell the lot for the Lord, and shall offer him as a sin-offering. But the goat upon which fell the lot for a Remover (of sins), shall be presented alive before the Lord for to make an atonement with (for) him, and for to send him away for a Remover (of sins) into the wilderness."

v. 26. "And he that sent away the goat for a Remover (of sins), shall wash his clothes and bathe his flesh in water, and afterward he shall come into the camp."

In the above renderings, the words "of sins" have been inserted after the word Remover for this reason, namely, that the use of the verb *ăzal*, from which the word rendered by "Remover" is derived, is confined in the Hebrew dialect to the single purpose or institution which is here under consideration; so that this particular word must have conveyed, to the mind of a Hebrew hearer or reader, this notion of a removal of *sins*, and none other.

8. It is further objected, that the word *azāzēl*, having no article, is probably a proper name. It seems not to have been noticed that when a verbal noun (or *nomen agentis*) is used to indicate a special office or function (to which class this word belongs), and has the preposition *lĕ* or *lă* prefixed to it, no article is used. For example:

I. Kings xix. 16. "Jehu shalt thou anoint *to be king* over Israel; and Elisha shalt thou anoint *to be prophet* in thy room" (lĕ-melek—lĕ-nāvī).

I. Samuel xxv. 30. "When the Lord shall have appointed thee *ruler* over Israel" (lĕ-nāgīd).

II. Samuel vii. 14. "I will be his father, and he shall be my son" (*lit.* I will be to him *for father*, and he shall be to me *for son*) (lĕ-āv—lĕ-vēn).

9. It is also contended that the preposition *la*, being prefixed alike to the two words indicating the objects or purposes of the two lots, must be taken to have one and the same meaning in both cases; that, therefore, if one is rendered "for the Lord," the other should be rendered "for Azazel."

As to this, it may suffice to point out that the recurrence of the *la* is simply an effect of the usage of the Jews in later times, according to which the word *Adonai* is substituted, in the public reading of the Hebrew text, for the ancient and true form of the Divine Name. The law of euphony in the Hebrew speech requires the same vowel-sound to be used before Adonai and 'Azazel. If the Divine Name had been read in its original form at the time when the Masoretic revision was made, the vowels would have been different in the two cases. Compare

Gen. xxxviii. 24. "It was told *(to) Judah*" (l-Ihūdah).

Gen. xl. 9. "The chief butler told his dream *to Joseph*" (lĕ-Yōsēf).

Nor would the inference be a sound one, even if the vowel of the preposition had been originally the same in both cases. The Hebrew prepositions are few, and are therefore used in many senses; but the *noun* before which the preposition is placed suffices to limit and fix the meaning in each case. So it is with ourselves. Consider in how many senses we use the preposition *for;* and that oftentimes even in the same sentence. Yet the *noun* to which the preposition is prefixed is such as to exclude all ambiguity. So the Hebrew preposition *lĕ* or *la*, immediately prefixed to a *nomen agentis*, that is to say, a word indicating the performer of some work or function, can have but one meaning, which in older English would be expressed by *for to be;* a meaning which, when prefixed to a proper name, even to the special Divine Name, it cannot have.

Nor is there anything extraordinary in the fact of this preposition being thus used in different senses in the same sentence. Thus—

Exodus xii. 24. "Ye shall observe this thing *for an ordinance to thee and to thy sons* for ever" (lĕ-χok lĕ-kā ū-lĕ-vānĕ-ka).

Here the preposition *lĕ* is prefixed alike to the *law* which is to be observed, and to the *persons* who are to observe it.

Levit. xxvi. 12. "I will be your God, and ye shall be my people:" *lit.* to you for a God—to me for a people (lā-kem l'Elōhīm—l-ī lĕ-ām).

Here the same preposition, with no other change than such as the rules of euphony require, is prefixed alike to the worshipper and to the object of worship. Compare Jerem. vii. 23; Ezek. xxxvi. 38.

10. The notion, accepted by some critics, that the word *'Azazel* was the designation of an evil spirit opposed to

the *Lord*, which spirit was to be propitiated by the offering of a goat, stands upon no evidence, and is entirely opposed to the spirit of the Mosaic legislation. It is rested on a supposed antithesis; which antithesis disappears as soon as it is perceived that the word was no proper name, but a common noun conveying in itself a meaning clear to every speaker of the Hebrew tongue. Besides, this view is inconsistent with the text. The goat, which is to be sent away into the wilderness, has been already presented before the Lord (v. 10); and that which is to secure the people against the return of the sin-bearing goat is not the death of the goat, but the nature of the place to which the goat is to be sent. That place is described in v. 22 by the words *ereṣ gĕzērāh*, i.e. a land cut off. The Hebrew root '*gāzar*'=secuit, dissecuit, is used to express the act of cutting in two (I. Kings iii. 25, 26); of dividing the Red Sea (Psalm cxxxvi. 13). In Arabic, the corresponding verb is *jazara*=amputavit, cecidit *racemos dactylorum maturorum*; the noun *jazīrah* means an island or an area insulated by rivers. In Syriac we have *gazīrθ-ō* and *gozarθ-ō* used in the same sense; and the root *gāzar*=abscidit, circumcidit (Castell) and its derivatives are used to represent περιτέμνειν and its derivatives.

The words, then, which are used in v. 22 to describe the land to which the goat is to be sent, properly describe a tract of land cut off on all sides, and completely isolated from the surrounding country, so as to render a return of the goat thence impossible.

11. It was natural that the goat should take his name from that symbolical act (*ă-zal-zal*) in which he was employed before the eyes of the people. It was equally natural, that whilst other derivatives of the root *zal* remained in use among the Hebrews, a derivative applied to a religious usage of special solemnity should cease to be used for other purposes.

12. If the view here taken be correct, there is no sufficient ground for the suggestion which has been put forward with a certain degree of authority, that it would be well to substitute the Hebrew word *Azazel* for the word *Scape Goat* in the text of our English version.

IV.

ON THE GRAMMATICAL STRUCTURE OF JOEL, Chap. ii.

1. The passage contained in vv. 15-20 of this chapter is very remarkable, as being one in which the Authorized Version departs from a clear and fundamental rule of the Hebrew language; to which rule, in cases out of number, our translators have adhered.

In this passage the particle *wa* is rendered, not as indicating a sequence of events in a narrative of the past, but as foreshowing an event to come to pass in a certain case. It is viewed as serving to link together two acts or events, both of which are, at the time of speaking, regarded by the speaker as future.

In a subsequent passage in the same chapter (v. 23) there occurs a similar departure from the rule.

2. The passage with which we are primarily concerned runs as follows in our Authorized Version:

"15. Blow the trumpet in Zion, sanctify a fast, call a solemn assembly:

"16. Gather the people, sanctify the congregation, assemble the elders, gather the children, and those that suck the breasts: let the bridegroom go forth of his chamber, and the bride out of her closet.

"17. Let the priests, the ministers of the Lord, weep between the porch and the altar, and let them say, Spare thy people, O Lord. . . . .

"18. Then will the Lord be jealous for his land, and pity his people.

"19. Yea, the Lord will answer, and say unto his people, Behold, I will send you corn, and wine, and oil, etc. . . .

"20. But I will remove far off from you the northern army, etc." . . .

The 18th verse and the portion of the 19th verse given above would, according to the usual practice of our translators, have been rendered thus:

"18. Then was the Lord jealous, and had pity on his people.

"19. And the Lord answered and said, Behold, I will send you corn, and wine, and oil, etc." . . .

3. In order to explain the course taken by our translators in this instance, it will be desirable to notice the renderings of the passage which lay before them in the two chief versions which had preceded their own, namely, the Septuagint and the Vulgate.

"Ἰωὴλ, κεφ. 2, vv. 15-20.

"15. σαλπίσατε σάλπιγγι ἐν Σιών, ἁγιάσατε νηστείαν, κηρύξατε θεραπείαν.

"16. συναγάγετε λαόν, ἁγιάσατε ἐκκλησίαν, ἐκλεξάσθε πρεσβυτέρους, συναγάγετε νήπια θηλάζοντα μαστούς, ἐξελθέτω νυμφίος ἐκ τοῦ κοιτῶνος αὐτοῦ καὶ νύμφη ἐκ τοῦ παστοῦ αὐτῆς.

"17. ἀνὰ μέσον τῆς κρηπῖδους τοῦ θυσιαστηρίου κλαύσονται οἱ ἱερεῖς οἱ λειτουργοῦντες τῷ Κυρίῳ καὶ ἐροῦσι Φεῖσαι, Κύριε, τοῦ λαοῦ σου. . . .

"18. καὶ ἐζήλωσε Κύριος τὴν γῆν αὐτοῦ καὶ ἐφείσατο τοῦ λαοῦ αὐτοῦ.

"19. καὶ ἀπεκρίθη Κύριος καὶ εἶπε τῷ λαῷ αὐτοῦ Ἰδοὺ, ἐγὼ ἔξαποστέλλω ὑμῖν τὸν σῖτον καὶ τὸν οἶνον καὶ τὸ ἔλαιον. . . .

"20. καὶ τὸν ἀπὸ βορρᾶ ἐκδιώξω ἀφ' ὑμῶν." . . .

"Joel, cap. ii. vv. 15-20.

"15. Canite tuba in Sion, sanctificate jejunium, vocate cætum.

"16. Congregate populum, sanctificate ecclesiam, coadunate senes, congregate parvulos et sugentes ubera; egrediatur sponsus de cubili suo et sponsa de talamo suo.

"17. Inter vestibulum et altare plorabunt sacerdotes ministri Domini et dicent; Parce, Domine, parce populo Tuo.

"18. Zelatus est Dominus terram suam et pepercit populo suo.

"19. Et respondit Dominus et dixit populo suo; Ecce, Ego mittam vobis frumentum et vinum et oleum, etc.

"20. Et eum qui ab aquilone est procul faciam a vobis."

It is to be noticed that, of these two old versions,

the later closely follows the earlier. Both take the verbs in v. 17 as referring to a future time; the verbs in vv. 18-19, as referring to a past time. Both agree in giving to the particle of sequence, in these last-named verses, its proper grammatical force.

Yet, in the version which both agree in giving, there is an obvious incongruity. For vv. 18-19 thus seem to state a sequence or consequence, in the past time, of an event which is still future. Our translators appear to have endeavoured to escape from this difficulty, by regarding the 17th verse as a continuation of the Imperative or Precative structure of the 16th, and so to have been led on to discover in vv. 18-19 a consequence —a *future* consequence—of the obedience (tacitly assumed) on the part of the people to the bidding in the vv. 15-16. In short, a misapprehension as to the grammatical structure of v. 17 led to a more serious misapprehension and to the infraction of a plain rule in vv. 18-19.

4. We proceed to consider, in the first place, the former of these misapprehensions.

The old versions had rightly regarded the verb in v. 17 as simply *indicative*, not *imperative* or *precative*, as asserting a fact; but had erred in assigning to that fact a future time. For the verb, being in the Imperfect, and without anything in the context to mark or suggest a future time, must be taken to indicate a present act.

All the difficulty disappears when it is observed that

Joel, Chap. II.

the sentence is an *inverted* one, and follows the rule by which such sentences are governed. The rule is this—When, in a statement of a fact, it is desired to give emphasis to some words which would ordinarily be placed after the main verb of the sentence, such words are brought forward to the beginning of the sentence, and the verb (in the Imperfect) is placed before the noun which indicates the agent or subject of the verb.

EXAMPLES.

I. Kings iii. 4. "A thousand burnt-offerings did Solomon offer." (Elef ȯlōθ ya‹aleh S.).

Deut. xxviii. 33. "The fruit of thy land—shall a nation, which thou knowest not, eat up." (pĕrī-admāθĕ-kā —yōkal ‹ām).

Psalm xxii. 1. "O Lord, in thy strength doth the king rejoice." (bĕ-‹ozzĕ-kā—yiśmaχmelek).

Amos vii. 11. "By the sword shall Jeroboam die." (ba-χerev yāmūθ Y.).

Proverbs xxiv. 3. "Through wisdom is a house builded" (bĕ-χokmāh yibbāneh bāyiθ).

N.B.—On the other hand, where a fact is announced without a stress being laid on any circumstance of the act, the noun stands before the verb.

Proverbs xiv. 11. "The house of the wicked shall be overthrown." (bēθ-rĕshā‹īm yissāmēd).

The inverted passage, therefore, in v. 17 (bēn hāūlām—yivkū kōhănīm) is to be read, not as a command or injunction, but as a description of an act; it being the purpose of the writer to give prominence in that description to the place wherein the act takes place.

5. If, then, we adhere to the rules of the Hebrew language, and at the same time follow the usage of the Authorized Version, and the habit of our English speech in treating Hebrew narratives as written throughout in words appropriated to the past time, the verses 17-19 of ch. ii. will be rendered as follows:

"17. Between the porch and the altar were the priests, the ministers of the Lord, weeping, saying, Spare thy people, O LORD, and give not thine heritage to reproach. . . .

"18. Then was the Lord jealous for his land, and pitied his people.

"19. Yea, the Lord answered and said, Behold, ..."

6. A similar correction is to be made in v. 23, which will run thus: "For he gave you the former rain moderately, and, after that, he causeth to come down the rain (shower)."

In order to render clear the structure of the verses 19-27 of this chapter, it is to be noticed that the Divine Voice, promising deliverance and blessing, is represented as speaking in vv. 19-20. In vv. 21-24 there is a pause or parenthesis, in which the prophet calls upon the people to lay aside fear, and to share his own overflowing thankfulness. Then the enumeration of promised blessings, which commenced in vv. 19-20, is resumed in v. 25, and carried on to the end of v. 27. This connexion is shown by the Perfects in these verses (sillamtī—ăkaltem—īda⸰tem) being *subjoined* to the Imperfect (arχīk̇) in v. 20, and so taking the future time thereof.

7. These points being settled, we will now endeavour to gain a clearer and more connected view of the whole structure of the earlier portion of this prophecy, conforming ourselves for this purpose to the Hebrew usage and idiom. It is to be observed, that there is nothing in the context to indicate that the events spoken of by the prophet are to take place at a future time. The Imperfect Form is therefore to be rendered throughout the narrative as a Present tense.

In ch. i. vv. 2-18, the prophet describes the strange spectacle which is before his eyes—the utter desolation of the land by the locust: the failure of food for man and beast; of the meat-offering and drink-offering for the worship of God. In his extreme distress, he despairs of help from man. "Unto thee, O LORD, do I cry. The beasts of the field also are crying unto Thee."

In ch. ii. vv. 1-11, the future form employed by our translators should be replaced throughout by a present. The prophet announces that the day of the Lord is come, is nigh at hand. He sets forth the awfulness of that day, the destruction wrought before his eyes by the terrible enemy that has invaded the land. Then the prophet reminds his brethren of the mercifulness of God, and moves them to turn to Him with all their heart.

While he is speaking, he hears a voice, as of one of the rulers of the people, proclaiming a solemn assembly. Straightway he sees before him, in the space between the altar of burnt-offering and the entrance of the temple, a group of priests weeping, and he hears their prayer, "Spare thy people, O LORD." Then he knows that the Lord hath pity upon the people; he even hears the words of divine promise.

8. An illustration of the form of narration, which we have been considering, may be found in the prophecy of Habakkuk. That prophet also relates a vision, wherein, in great distress of mind, he cries to God, complaining of the violence and iniquity of the people of the land. In vv. 2–4 the prophet speaks, in vv. 5–11 the Lord answers. Again, in i. 12–ii. 1, the prophet speaks. In the next verse (ii. 2) we meet the words *wai-yaʿăn-ēnī* Y.=the same phrase as in Joel ii. 19 (wai-yaʿan); which, in this instance, is rendered by our translators in strict conformity with the grammatical rule, "And the Lord answered me, and said." Yet the whole narration up to this point has been conducted merely by a recital of words spoken and answered, stated in the order in which they are conceived to have been spoken and answered. There has been no express indication of a past time; not even a statement of a fact: nothing more than a setting forth of words of complaint, of words in answer, and then of words of renewed complaint; whereupon follows immediately the verse ii. 2.

It appears therefore that there is no reason for regarding the passage in Joel as involving an exception to the recognized rule of the Hebrew language.

9. It may be added that a like departure from the grammatical rule occurs in our version of Habakkuk iii. 19. "The Lord God is my strength, and *He will make* my feet like hinds' feet, and *He will make* me to walk." Rather say, "So He maketh my feet like hinds' feet, and maketh me to walk upon my high places."

V.

ON SOME USES OF THE PARTICLE $e\theta$.

OF this particle one use is well known, and open to no question; namely, its use in pointing out the *object* of a transitive verb in its active form, or (which in effect is the same thing) the *subject* of such verb in its passive form. Of these two modes of employment, the former is the ordinary one, and occurs continually; the latter presents itself occasionally, *e.g.* in Exod. xxv. 28, Numb. xxxii. 5, Psalm lxxii. 19.

But there are other cases in which this particle is employed, as to which there is little agreement. It may be worth while to consider whether these, or at least one class of them, may not be found to fall within the operation of some general principle.

1. It is here proposed to notice those instances in which this particle is placed after an *intransitive* verb; or after a form of words which, for this purpose, may be regarded as equivalent to an intransitive verb. Such forms are:

a. Those where a transitive verb having been used, the *object* of that verb has also been expressly stated.

44   *The Particle eθ.*

b. Those where a reflective form of the verb has been used.

In such cases the object of the verb being already given, either by express statement or as being involved in the verb itself, the *eθ* which follows cannot be intended to denote the object. For what purpose then is it used?

2. Our inquiry cannot start better than from a passage in which the intransitive verb used is one of the simplest and plainest in point of meaning, and where the context is also singularly clear and full. Such is the following:

II. Kings vi. 1–4. "And the sons of the prophets said unto Elisha, Behold now, the place where we dwell with thee is too strait for us. Let us go, we pray thee, unto Jordan. . . . and let us make a place there where we may dwell. And he answered, Go ye. And one said, Be content, I pray thee, and go *with thy servants.* And he said, I will go. So he went *with them.*" (eθ—itt-ām).

In this passage it is obvious that the movement of Elisha is dependent on that of the sons of the prophets. His action follows theirs; it continues throughout to be guided and determined by theirs, and to depend thereon.

Other examples are the following:

Genesis xiii. 5. "Lot also, which went *with Abram.*" (eθ-Avrām).

Genesis xxiv. 40. "The Lord will send his angel

with thee, and will prosper thy way." (itt-āk) *i.e.* he shall follow thy movements throughout the journey.

Genesis xxvi. 24. "Fear not, for I am (will be) *with thee* and will bless thee." (ittĕ-ka), *i.e.* whithersoever thou goest my blessing shall accompany thee.

Genesis xxviii. 4. "God give thee the blessing of Abraham, to thee and to *thy seed with thee*" (itt-āk-), *i.e.* following thee and sharing in thy fortunes. The LXX. renders the words by τῷ σπέρματί σου μετὰ σὲ.

Genesis xxxvii. 2. "Joseph, being seventeen years old, was feeding his flock *with* his brethren; and the lad was *with* the sons of Bilhāh, and *with* the sons of Zilpah" (eθ—eθ—eθ): *i.e.* in feeding the flock, he travelled along with his brethren, moving as they moved.

Genesis xxxix. 2. "And the Lord was *with* Joseph, and he was a prosperous man" (eθ), *i.e.* wherever he went, the blessing of God followed him.

Genesis v. 22. "Enoch *walked with God*." (yiθhallēk eθ-hā-Elōhīm); *lit.* set himself to walk, *i.e.* guided his conduct, in accordance with God's will.

3. Again, we find eθ used in respect of the mutual action of two men, or two parties of men—*e.g.* in case of war or litigation; that is to say, when the action of one person or party depends on, or is determined by, that of the other.

Genesis xiv. 8. "They joined battle *with them* in the vale of Siddīm" (itt-ām).

Prov. xxiii. 11–12. "Enter not into the fields of

the fatherless: for their redeemer is mighty; he shall plead their cause *with thee*" (itt-āk), *i.e.* the act of the redeemer or avenger shall follow upon the act of the wrongdoer.

4. Sometimes the notion of following or accompanying is lost in the more general idea of dependence, of being in the power or under the charge of another person.

Genesis vii. 23. "Noah only remained alive, and they that were *with him* in the ark." (itt-ō), *i.e.* not merely who were there at the same time and place, but who had followed his guidance thither, were under his care.

Genesis xxx. 29, 30. "Thou knowest how I have served thee, and how thy cattle was *with me*. For it was little which thou hadst before I came, and it is now increased unto a multitude." (itt-ī), *i.e.* under my care and management.

Genesis xliii. 8–9. "And Judah said unto Israel his father, Send the lad *with me*. . . . I will be surety for him; of my hand shalt thou require him." (ītt-ī), *i.e.* the lad is to follow his brother's guidance, to conform himself to his brother's directions; in which case, his brother will be responsible for him.

Levit. xix. 13. "The wages of him that is hired shall not abide *with thee* all night until the morning." (itt-āk), *i.e.* shall not remain in thy keeping and in thy power to dispose of them.

Numbers i. 3–5. "Thou and Aaron shalt number them by their armies. And *with you* there shall be a man of every tribe. And these are the names of the men that shall stand *with you*" (ittĕ-kem—ittĕ-kem), *i.e.* these persons shall be subordinate to you, following your movements, acting under your direction.

II. Kings x. 2-3. "Seeing your master's sons are *with you*, and there are *with you* chariots and horses, a fenced city also, and armour; look out the best and meetest of your master's sons, and fight for your master's house" (ittĕ-kem—ittĕ-kem).

Leviticus xix. 33. "If a stranger sojourn *with thee* in your land, ye shall not vex him" (ittĕ-kā), *i.e.* if a stranger comes to seek a home for himself in thy land, and so puts himself in thy power, deal kindly with him.

Job xiv. 5. "Seeing his days are determined, the number of his months are *with thee;* thou hast appointed his bounds that he cannot pass" (itt-āk).

5. Sometimes eθ is used of the appertaining of one *thing* to another.

I. Samuel vi. 15. "The Levites took down the ark of the Lord, and the coffer that was *with it*, wherein the jewels of gold were." (itt-ō). Comp. vv. 3-4.

6. In Genesis xl. is a remarkable passage where the secondary and dependent action or movement, and that also upon which it depends or from which it arises, are conceived of as taking place in the mind of one person. (vv. 13-14) "Yet within three days shall Pharaoh . . . restore thee unto thy place. . . *But think on me* when

it shall be well with thee" (kī im zĕkarta-nī ittĕ-kā). The LXX. appear to have rightly apprehended the force of *eθ* in this case. They render the Hebrew words by ἀλλὰ μνήσθητί μου διὰ σεαυτοῦ, *i.e.* When thou shalt be restored unto thy place, remember me *by thyself, i.e. by the action of thine own mind.* Thy restored prosperity will naturally recall to thy mind, by way of contrast, this prison and me.

7. It appears, then, that, as *eθ* is used after a transitive verb to indicate the person *towards whom* the action of the verb is directed; so, after an intransitive verb, *eθ* is used to indicate the person *by whom* the action of the verb is guided or determined, the person on whom it depends.

VI.

THE DIVINE NAME.

The Hebrew Name, which in our Version of the Old Testament is translated "the Lord," has been in recent times otherwise rendered by many scholars, English and foreign, who agree in treating it as equivalent to "the Eternal." The object of the present inquiry is to ascertain the true meaning and import of that Name.

1. It is known that the Jews, at the beginning of the Christian era, had lost the ancient pronunciation of this Name. Fearing to take the Divine Name in vain or to utter it irreverently, they thought it safer not to utter it at all. Accordingly, in the public reading of the Scripture, another name was substituted, namely '*Adonai*,' that is to say, *Lord*. In conformity with this usage, the Alexandrine translators expressed the Divine Name by ὁ Κύριος.

The original Name, however, was not removed from the text: the consonants of that Name were left standing; but, instead of the proper vowel-points, those of the word

Adonai were introduced; with only one alteration, which was rendered necessary by the rules of the Hebrew language. The vowel-mark which stands under the first letter of the word Adonai (equivalent to *ă*) cannot, consistently with those rules, be placed under the first letter of the Divine Name. It was therefore replaced by the vowel-mark which is here represented by *ĕ*. Further, in consistency with the same usage, the vowel-points belonging to certain prepositions or particles, prefixed in the Hebrew text to the Divine name, were altered so as to adapt them to the word *Adonai*.

There are cases where the word 'Adonai' occurs in the Hebrew text immediately before the Divine Name. In such cases, to prevent repetition, the word 'Elohim' was substituted for the Divine Name.

So it came to pass that when, after the revival of learning, Western scholars, ignorant or heedless of the Jewish usage, began to read the Hebrew Scriptures for themselves, they pronounced the Divine Name just as they found it written. Thus was introduced the name *Jehovah* (or *Yehovah*): which (to borrow the terse language of a living scholar) " is a name made up of the consonants of one word and the vowels of another."—(*Prophecy a Preparation for Christ*, Lect. 2.) [1]

---

[1] "The popular pronunciation, '*Jehovah*,' is altogether a mistake. When a word in the text is not read (and this ceased to be read before the vowels were written), the vowels belong, not to the word itself, but to another, which is to be substituted for it. . . . The placing of the vowels under the word is an indication, not that they *are* to be used with the word, but that they are *not* to be used with it."—Dr. Pusey on Hosea xii. 5.

2. As to the true and original pronunciation of the Divine Name, some direct evidence has been discovered by scholars. Theodoret, a Syrian bishop (who died about the middle of the fifth century), tells us that the Samaritans (who appear not to have shared in the Jewish feeling against uttering the word) pronounced the Name as Ιαβέ. In this Ιαβέ, the first letter represents the Yōd, the third the Vau of the Hebrew name. The *a* and the ε represent the original vowels of the first and second syllables. The Greek language furnished no means of representing the *h*, with which each of the Hebrew syllables ended.

This evidence is strengthened by inferences derived from the structure of the language itself. Various names of kings and prophets occur in the Old Testament, in which the Divine Name is incorporated with some other word to form the name of a man. Sometimes the Divine Name appears as the latter, sometimes as the former part, of the human name. Thus we have Aχazyāhū (Ahaziah), χizkīyāhū (Hezekiah), Yesa*i*yāhū (Isaiah), Yirmyāhū (Jeremiah). Again, we have Yĕhōnāθān or Yōnāθān (Jonathan), Yĕhōsāfā*t* or Yōsāfā*t* (Jehoshaphat). In the former class we recognize the Divine Name as *Yahweh:* the same change having taken place in the latter syllable, as that which takes place in the often cited instance of 'yistaχū' for 'yistaχaweh,' from the root '*sāχ*āh.' And the analogy is closer still in the frequent cases where *chych, tihyeh,* and *yihyeh,* following the particle *wa,* become *ehī, tĕhī,* and *yehī:* the syllable *yeh* being in these cases reduced to the single vowel *ī,* just as in those proper names *weh* is reduced to *ū*. In the latter class of names the long vowel of the first syllable has been shortened into ĕ, a change which takes place frequently in the first syllable of Hebrew words whenever syllables are added on at the end, *e.g.* 'dĕvārīm' from 'dāvār.'

In certain Psalms (Ps. cxi.-cxiii., cxvii., cxlvi.-cl.) we find a shorter form of the Divine Name. The Psalmist calls on his hearers to join in the hymn which he is chanting: *Praise ye the Lord.* "Hallĕlū-yāh." And this shorter name seems to have been appropriated to this use. "*Extol Him by His name Yah, and rejoice before Him*" (Ps. lxviii. 4). Now this *Yāh* is a regular abbreviation of *Yahweh*, the loss of the latter syllable being compensated by a lengthening of the syllable that is retained.

3. This word *Yahweh* (more commonly written *Yahveh*) is a part of the verb *hāwāh* or *hāvāh*, being the third person singular of the Imperfect of the Causative form of that verb. And this verb *hāwāh* is only an older form of the verb which in the Hebrew text appears generally as *hāyāh*. In the structure of the Hebrew language there are indications of changes having taken place in course of time, whereby a Vau which existed in older grammatical forms has been replaced in more recent forms by a Yōd. Thus, in various parts of the conjugation of certain verbs which in Hebrew begin with a Yōd, there are signs, not to be mistaken, that such verbs once began in Hebrew, as they now begin in Arabic, with a Vau. Thus, from the Hebrew root

yālad (Arab. *walada*), we find derivatives *hōlīd* and its passive *hūlad, nōlad, yivvāléd*, etc., all of which are manifestly to be traced to an older root *wālad*. In the Divine Name the archaic mode of writing would naturally be retained. But it is not absolutely confined to that name. In the patriarchal blessing, "*Be thou Lord over thy brethren* " (Gen. xxvii. 29), the primitive form *hĕwēh* is found, not the modern *hĕyēh*.

Another example of the like change is furnished by the Hebrew root χ*āyāh* (*to live*) and its derivative χ*ayyāh* (*to cause to live, give life*), which in the corresponding Arabic and Syriac forms retain the *w* throughout. In this case, the archaic form, abandoned in the ordinary language, is found unchanged in the name of the "mother of all living," χ*awwāh* or χ*avvāh*, Gen. iii. 20.

4. The commonly received interpretation of this name is clearly stated by M. Nicolas (*Etudes Critiques sur la Bible*, Paris, 1862, pp. 118-119). "*Jahveh* dérive du verbe *havah* ou *hajah*, dont il est un futur pris substantivement. Il signifie par conséquent *ens*, l'être qui existe toujours, tandis que tous les autres êtres sont soumis au changement et à la mort; l'être qui est par lui-même, par sa propre vertu, tandis que les êtres créés n'existent que par des causes indépendantes d'eux. C'est donc l'existence absolue, l'être existant par lui-même, que le terme *Jahveh* exprime ; il ne saurait rester le moindre doute à ce sujet."

In support of this interpretation, certain Greek Fathers

of the Church have often been cited. But their authority can hardly be regarded as conclusive. We do not appear to have any grounds for believing those Fathers (with the doubtful exception of Origen) to have been well acquainted with the Hebrew tongue. Their opinion on this point seems to resolve itself into their acceptance of the Alexandrine Version of the Old Testament, which was regarded by them as possessing a very eminent degree of authority, if not as actually inspired.[1] The Divine Name, as given in Exodus iii. 14, is rendered in that Version, by ὁ Ὤν.

Ewald speaks less decidedly than M. Nicolas. His words are, "That *Yahveh* is the Deliverer, is the teaching of the whole Pentateuch, as well as of the preamble to the Ten Commandments."—*History of the People of Israel* (Martineau), vol. ii. p. 110 *n*. Elsewhere he says, "The name *Yahveh* has in Hebrew no clear etymology,"—and again, "The word (if of the same root as *hāyāh*) might denote 'the Existing, *i.e.* the Real, the Permanent, the Eternal.'"—*Ibid.* pp. 155, 158.

5. We now proceed to collect and classify examples of the use of the root *hāyāh*, and so to determine the original force and meaning thereof.

a. Where it is used in the sense of *to happen—befall—come to pass*:

Genesis xxix. 23. "*Then it cometh to pass in the evening,*

---

[1] Bleek, *Introduction to the Old Testament* (Venables), volume ii. page 410.

that he taketh Leah," lit. Then there *befalleth* (a time) in the evening, *then* he taketh (wa-ihī—wai-yi*kk*aχ).

Judges xiv. 15. "And it came to pass on the seventh day, that they said," lit. Then *there befalleth* (a time) in the seventh day, *then* they say, etc. (wa-ihī—wai-yōmĕrū).

I. Sam. i. 4. "And when the time was that Elkanah offered, he gave," etc. *lit.* Then *happeneth the day, so* Elkanah offereth (wa-ihī hai-yōm, wai-yizbaχ E.).

The LXX. render the words καὶ ἐγενήθη ἡμέρα καὶ ἔθυσεν.

I. Sam. xiv. 1. "Now it came to pass upon a day, that Jonathan said," *lit.* Then *happeneth the day, then saith* Jonathan (wa-ihī hai-yōm, wai yōmer); and again, in precisely the same form of words, in II. Kings, chapter iv. verses 8–11 and 18.

I. Kings xiii. 32. "For the saying shall *surely come to pass*" (hāyōh yihyeh).

I. Sam. vi. 9. "It was a chance that *happened* to us." (hāyāh).

Judges x. 3. "The spirit of the Lord *came upon him.*" (tehī).

b. Where it is used to express a transition or change from one condition to another, or the assumption of some special relation or character:

Gen. xxxiv. 15. "If you will *become* as we" (tihyū).

Exodus vii. 19, "That they may *become* blood" (yihyū).

II. Sam. viii. 6. "The Syrians (*lit.* Aram) *became* servants to David" (tĕhī).

II. Sam. xi. 27. "She *became* his wife" (tĕhī).

Judges xviii. 4. "Then he hired me and *I became* his priest" (ehī).

Leviticus xxvi. 3-12. "If ye walk in my statutes and keep my commandments and do them, then will I walk among you and *will be your God, and ye shall be my people*" (wĕ-hāyīθi—wĕ-attem tihyū).

Psalm cxviii. 22. "The stone, which the builders rejected, *is become* the head stone of the corner" (hāyĕθāh).

c. Where it is used to express the amount of several sums added together:

Exodus xxxviii. 24. "All the gold that was occupied for the work in all the work of the holy place *was* twenty and nine talents and seven hundred and thirty shekels" (wa-ihī).

d. Where it is used to indicate a quality or state, physical or moral, existing at a certain time:

Genesis i. 2. "The earth *was without form* and void" (hāyĕθāh).

Jonah iii. 3. "Now Nineveh *was an exceeding great city*" (hāyĕθāh).

Genesis xxix. 17. "Rachel *was beautiful* and well favoured" (hāyĕθāh).

Deut. iii. 4. "There *was not* a city which we took not" (lō hāyĕθāh); *i.e.* there was no city *of such a description or nature as to be able to withstand* our attack. *Vulgate:* Non fuit oppidum *quod nos effugeret.*

I. Sam. iv. 9. "Be strong *and quit yourselves like men*" (hĕyū la-ănāsim).

I. Sam. xviii. 17. "*Be thou valiant* for me" (hĕyēh lĕ-ven-χayil).

e. Where it is used to express a temporary relation, as of one neighbour to another, or of property to its owner:

II. Sam. xii. 2-3. "There were two men in one city: the one rich and the other poor. The rich man had (*lit.* to the rich man *belonged*) exceeding many flocks and herds" (hāyāh).

II. Kings xxiv. 7. "All the land that *pertained* to the king of Egypt" (hāyĕθāh).

Upon a review of these examples it appears that the state or relation which is expressed by the root *hāyāh* is a temporary and variable one; one which begins, changes, and ceases, not one which ever abides unchanged. All the uses of this root may be readily traced back to that which is assigned to it, as its original meaning, by Professor W. Wright. "The Hebrew and Aramaic 'hāwā, hāyā, hawā, hawō,' is originally 'cecidit' (Arabic hawā, 'decidit'), then 'accidit, evenit, factus est, fuit.'"— (*Society of Biblical Archæology*, vol. iii. p. 106.)

The result then of our inquiry is, that the common interpretation of the Divine Name assumes for the root 'hāwāh' or 'hāyāh' a meaning, for which (common as the word is) no authority is produced. No instance is found in which it is used in the sense of *real being, absolute unchangeable existence.*

6. The Hebrew language is not without a word to express *actual* presence or existence. That word is yēs. The meaning therefore of yēs approaches more nearly to that which is ascribed to hāwāh, but it is far from including the sense of *absolute* or *immutable* existence.

Genesis xliv. 26. "If our youngest brother *be with us,* then will we go down" (im-yēs—itt-ānū).

Numbers xiii. 20. "Whether *there be* wood therein or not" (hă-yēs).

Judges vi. 13. "*If the Lord be* (really) *with us,* why then is all this befallen us?" (wĕ-yēs Y. ʻimm-ānū).

I. Sam. xx. 8. "*If there be in me* iniquity" (im yes-b-ī).

I. Sam. xxi. 9. "*Is there* not *here* under thy hand spear or sword?" (yes-pōh).

Psalm xiv. 2. "The Lord looked down from heaven upon the children of men, to see *if there were any* that did understand" (hă-yēs).

Psalm lviii. 12. "Verily *there is a God* that judgeth in the earth" (yes-Elōhīm).

7. We have now arrived at the true meaning of the verb 'hāwāh' or 'hāyāh.' It *indicates* the occurrence of an event, or the appearance of an object, as part of an historical series. It does not assert anything about the mode of existence of the object; least of all does it assert an unchangeable or absolute existence. The *Hifil* form

of the same verb expresses, not the causing a thing to exist, in the sense of creating it, but the causing some phenomenon or event or state of things to happen or become manifest. As applied to God, it would indicate an act, not of Creation, but of Providence.

But 'Jahveh' is a proper name. It cannot (as the words *El* or *Elōhīm* can) take a possessive pronoun after it, or an article before it. It is agreed on all sides that the Divine Name (like all other Hebrew names) had a significance. Can we ascertain, what the precise significance was?

We find in the Hebrew Scriptures various kinds of proper names. In some instances the name of a man is formed from the third person singular of the Imperfect of a verb. The name so given had reference to some act of the person to whom it was given, or to some act connected with that person. Accordingly the verbal form which expressed such act was taken and (after a slight modification in some cases) converted into a proper name. Thus from yiṣχak (*he laughs*) was derived the proper name Yiṣχāk (Isaac), Genesis xvii. 17, and xxi. 6. Yaʿakov (*he taketh by the heel*) became the name of another patriarch, Genesis xxv. 26. Many similar names occur, though without any indication of the circumstances which led to their being given. Such are Yiftāχ (Jephthah) from yiftaχ "*he opens*"; Yibχār (Ibhar) from yibχar "*he chooseth*," II. Sam. v. 15; Yimlā (Imlah), "*he filleth*," I. Kings xxii. 8. Another set of names is taken from the third person singular of the Imperfect of the *Causative* form of the Verb. Such are Yāīr (Jair) "*he causeth to shine*"; Yamlēk (Jamlech) "*he causeth to reign*," I. Chron. iv. 34; Yaflēt (Japhlet) "*he delivereth*," I. Chron. vii. 33.

It may therefore be inferred that this Name for the Divine Being referred, in its origin, to some manifestation of Divine Power ordering the course of events.

8. In some parts of the Law (particularly in the Book of Leviticus) we find, at the close of a denunciation, or of a commandment, one or other of these two forms of words: "I am the Lord," or "I am the Lord your God." These words appear to be added simply for the purpose of ensuring the obedience due to divine authority. But we sometimes meet with a phrase which appears to have a different significance, namely: "*Ye (or they) shall know that I am the Lord.*"

If the Name (Yahveh) which we render 'Lord' was, as its structure shows it to have been, a word clearly significant in the ears of a Hebrew, we should expect in such cases to find in the context something from which that significance might be gathered. With a view to determine (so far as this method may guide us) what that significance is, we now proceed to pass in review the passages in which this form of words occurs.

Exod. vi. 7. "Ye shall know that I am the Lord your God, *which bringeth you out from under the burdens of the Egyptians.*"

Exod. vii. 5. "The Egyptians shall know that I am

the Lord, *when I stretch forth my hand upon Egypt and bring out the children of Israel from among them.*"

Ibid. 17. "In this thou shalt know that I am the Lord: behold, *I will smite upon the waters* which are in the river, and they shall be turned to blood."

Exod. viii. 22. "*I will sever in that day* the land of Goshen in which my people dwell — to the end thou mayest know that I am the Lord."

Exod. x. 2. "That thou mayest tell in the ears of thy son, and of thy son's son, *what things I have wrought in Egypt*, and my signs which I have done among them; that ye may know how that I am the Lord."

Exod. xiv. 4. "*I will be honoured upon Pharaoh and upon all his host*, that the Egyptians may know that I am the Lord."

Ibid. 18. "And the Egyptians shall know that I am the Lord, *when I have gotten me honour upon Pharaoh*, upon his chariots and upon his horsemen."

I. Kings xx. 13. "Hast thou seen this great multitude? Behold, I *will deliver it into thy hand* this day; and thou shalt know that I am the Lord."

Isaiah xlix. 22-23. "Behold, *I will lift up my hand to the gentiles*, and set up my standard to the people;— and kings shall be thy nursing fathers, and their queens thy nursing mothers; they shall bow down to thee, and thou shalt know that I am the Lord; for they shall not be ashamed that wait for me."

Jeremiah xxiv. 6-7. "I will set mine eyes upon them (that are carried captive out of Judah) for good, and

I will bring them again to this land;—and I will give them a heart to know me, that I am the Lord."

Ezekiel vi. 3-7. "Behold, I, *even I, will bring a sword upon you, and I will destroy your high places;* and your altars shall be desolate and your images shall be broken; and I will cast down your slain men before your idols.—And the slain shall fall in the midst of you, and ye shall know that I am the Lord."

Ezek. vii. 3-4. "Now is the end come upon thee, and *I will send mine anger upon thee and will judge thee according to thy ways,* and will recompense upon thee all thine abominations;—and ye shall know that I am the Lord."

Ezek. xii. 15. "And they shall know that I am the Lord, *when I shall scatter them among the nations* and disperse them in the countries."

Ezek. xx. 42. "Ye shall know that I am the Lord, *when I shall bring you into the land of Israel,* into the country for the which I lifted up my hand to give it to your fathers."

Ezek. xxxvii. 11-14. "Son of man, these bones are the whole house of Israel; behold, they say, our bones are dried and our hope is lost.—Behold, O my people, I will open your graves, and cause you to come up out of your graves, and bring you into the land of Israel. And ye shall know that I am the Lord, *when I have opened your graves and brought you up out of your graves,* and shall put my spirit in you, and ye shall live, and I shall place you in your own land: then shall ye know that I the Lord have spoken it and performed it."

The passages already cited are in number about one-fifth of the passages of the Old Testament in which the phrase under consideration occurs. The remaining four-fifths lead us to the same conclusion as to the significance of this form of words.

These passages point, not to the eternity or to the absolute existence of God, but to His dealings with men; to some special manifestations of Divine power in the moral government of the world, either by way of visitation and judgment or by way of mercy and deliverance.

9. This signification of the Divine Name is also suitable to the context in the remarkable passage of Exod. vi. 2-8. "*I am Yahveh* (He that bringeth things to pass—the orderer of events—the God of Providence). *And so, I appeared from time to time to Abraham, to Isaac, and to Jacob, in* (the name of) *God Almighty, but* (in) *my Name Yahveh was I not known to them. I also established my covenant with them to give to them the land of Canaan: And I also heard the groaning of the children of Israel, and then I remembered my covenant. Therefore say—I am Yahveh, and I will bring you forth from under the burdens of the Egyptians, and rid you out of their bondage, and redeem you and take you to me for a people, and be to you for a God. And* (by the deliverance which I shall have wrought for you) *ye shall know that I am Yahveh your God, which bringeth you out—and I will bring you in unto the land—.*" This passage may be regarded as an explanation or exemplification of the meaning of the Divine Name.

10. In Exodus iii. 13-14 we find another passage of great importance in reference to this question. "And Moses said unto God, when I come unto the children of Israel, and shall say unto them, The God of your fathers hath sent me unto you; and they shall say to me, what is his name? What shall I say unto them? And God said unto Moses, I AM THAT I AM; and He said, Thus shalt thou say unto the children of Israel, I AM hath sent me unto you." In the Hebrew text the words, which are translated *I am that I am*, stand thus, 'Ehyeh, aser ehyeh.' The verb, which occurs in them twice, is also derived from the root 'hāyāh': being the first person of the Imperfect form of that root. It will be observed, that in this passage the verb takes its later form 'hāyāh,' instead of 'hāwāh.' For the name here given did not become the recognized special name of God, and therefore was not sheltered by religious awe from the ordinary course of change. Still it was a *name*, as Hebrews understood the word *name*, *i.e.* it conveyed to them some meaning which might fitly serve to mark the character of the object of their worship. And in this case we have no difficulty in determining what that meaning was.

For the use of this word either in its full form *ehyeh*, or in the shorter form *ĕhī* (which it usually takes when preceded by the particle *wa*), is not infrequent. Thus:

Judges xii. 9. "And Jephthah said, If ye bring me home again to fight against the children of Ammon, and the Lord deliver them before me, *shall I be* (become) your head?" (ehyeh).

II. Sam. vii. 8-9. "I took thee from following the sheep to be ruler over my people;—*Then* (after that) *I was with thee* whithersoever thou wentest—and I cut off all thine enemies" (wā-ehyeh). Here ehyeh expresses a certain relation of God to a man—a relation of guidance and protection.

Psalm cii. 8. "I watch, and *I am as a sparrow* alone upon the house-top" (wā-ehyeh).

Psalm xxxviii. 15. "Thus *I was* (became) *as a man* that heareth not" (wā-ehī).

Psalm l. 21. "Thou hast thought that *I was altogether such a one as thyself*," *i.e.* in mind and moral character (ehyōθ-ehyeh).

The word ehyeh, then, indicates a condition, character, or relation subsisting at some definite time, beginning or continuing at that time. In no case is it found to express "I am," in the sense of absolute existence.

The meaning to be given to the words Ehyeh aser ehyeh,' if we guide ourselves by the evidence furnished by the Hebrew books, may be paraphrased in this way: "*I show myself from time to time, even as I show myself.* I stand from time to time in varying relations to men. This is my *name*. Only from my dealings with men, is my character to be apprehended by men."

No better commentary on this name can be given than that which the Book of Exodus itself supplies, in the passage xxxiv. 5-7. "And the Lord descended, and proclaimed the *name* of the Lord. And the Lord passed by before him (Moses) and proclaimed 'the Lord,' the Lord

God, merciful and gracious, long suffering and abundant in goodness and truth; keeping mercy for thousands, forgiving iniquity and transgression and sin—and that will by no means clear the guilty; visiting the iniquity of the fathers upon the children, and upon the children's children unto the third and to the fourth generation." Here the "name" of God is a setting-forth of what God is in his relation to man; of what he is in that character with which we are chiefly concerned, namely, that of our moral governor.

11. This view of the Divine Name, to which we are led by the evidence of the Hebrew language itself, is in full conformity with the general religious teaching of the Old Testament, which is practical and moral; setting forth, in a form readily intelligible, the character of God in His relations to man. It does not concern itself with those problems, which philosophy has been ever vainly seeking to solve. It addresses itself to human needs and human duties, and not to abstract inquiries. Not that the highest abstract truths were unknown or untaught. Lawgiver, and Prophet, and Psalmist, set before the people the greatness and the eternity of God in language most clear and impressive. Yet the Name whereby He was put before them as the object of their daily worship, was not one which would exalt Him to the utmost above the frail and changeful and transitory lives of His worshippers, and thereby remove Him far away from them into the height of a Being beyond man's search or

comprehension; but rather a Name which should bring Him nigh to them, as One ever mindful of them, ever carrying forward His great purpose for their good, working for them deliverance in every time of need: as One whose Providence ordereth all things in Heaven and on earth.

12. If the reasoning of this essay be correct, if this Name did convey to the mind of a Hebrew hearer the thought above expressed, it follows that the old rendering —'Adōnāi,' Κύριος or *Lord*, is to be preferred to that which has of late been substituted for it.

www.ingramcontent.com/pod-product-compliance
Lightning Source LLC
Chambersburg PA
CBHW020335090426
42735CB00009B/1544